A DOG'S LIFE

CREATIVE EDUCATION CREATIVE PAPERBACKS

Published by Creative Education and Creative Paperbacks
P.O. Box 227, Mankato, Minnesota 56002
Creative Education and Creative Paperbacks
are imprints of The Creative Company
www.thecreativecompany.us

Design and production by Chelsey Luther
Art direction by Rita Marshall
Printed in the United States of America

Photographs by Alamy (Mary H. Swift), Dreamstime
(Chalermphon Kumchai), Getty Images (Robert Daly/
Caiaimage), iStockphoto (adogslifephoto, BLACKDAY,
cirano83, FatCamera, Dorottya_Mathe, Mkovalevskaya,
PeopleImages), Shutterstock (9dream studio, Aurora72,
CNuisin, M.Stasy, mariait, Bachkova Natalia,
vectorOK, WilleeCole Photography, Dora Zett)

Library of Congress Cataloging-in-Publication Data
Names: Rosen, Michael J., author.
Title: Handling your dog / Michael J. Rosen.
Series: A dog's life.
Summary: An instructional guide to handling dogs, this title
touches on how to pet, lift, and groom a dog and informs
young dog owners what to expect from the loyal, loving
animals.

Identifiers: ISBN 978-1-64026-054-2 (hardcover) / ISBN 978-
1-62832-642-0 (pbk) / ISBN 978-1-64000-170-1 (eBook)
This title has been submitted for CIP processing under LCCN
2018938981.

CCSS: RI.1.1, 2, 4, 5, 6, 7; RI.2.1, 2, 5, 6, 7; RI.3.1, 5, 7; RF.1.1, 3, 4;
RF.2.3, 4

First Edition HC 9 8 7 6 5 4 3 2 1
First Edition PBK 9 8 7 6 5 4 3 2 1

HANDLING
Your Dog

CONTENTS

If Your Dog Could Read ...

You will have to read these six books for your dog as well as yourself. You will be both student and teacher. A dog is a fine student—*if* you are a fine teacher!

Your dog will supply his talent to learn. He will work for praise, play, and treats because they create safety, happiness, and comfort.

In this book, you will learn the kinds of touch a dog most enjoys. Your hands can provide a secure lift. They can offer a soothing touch, a healthful massage, and a relaxing grooming. These all deepen the relationship you share with your four-legged companion.

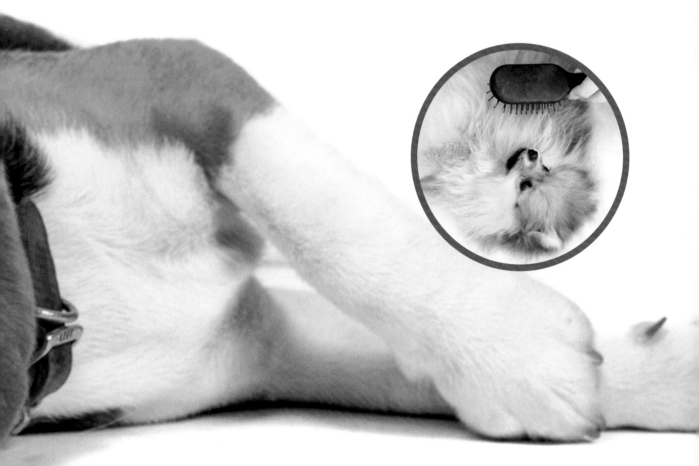

Safety First

When you need to lift or carry a dog, fully support him in your arms. Never lift a dog that is too heavy or squirmy to hold securely. If the dog struggles, squat down and release him.

CORRECT

The safest way to lift a dog is to first squat down. Slip one arm under the dog's chest. Support the front half of his body in your elbow. Hold the leg that is not against your chest in your hand. Place your other arm under the dog's rear end. Scoop up, resting his hind legs in your elbow. Stand slowly, using your legs.

To return the dog to the ground, squat down. Set the dog's rear legs on the ground, and then lower the front legs.

❌ INCORRECT

Soothing Spots

A relaxed dog will lean in to your strokes, pawing you to continue. But if he shrinks down, moves away, or makes any whines or grumbles—stop! He is not enjoying your touch.

Dogs typically like to be scratched on the chest and belly, under the collar, or along the lower back. Try rubbing behind or along the outer ears. Gently scratch the top of the head, between the eyes, and under the jaw.

On your dog's belly, right below the ribs before the hips, there is an especially soothing spot. If your dog acts anxious—say, in the car or at the vet's office— rub this spot gently, and speak reassuringly.

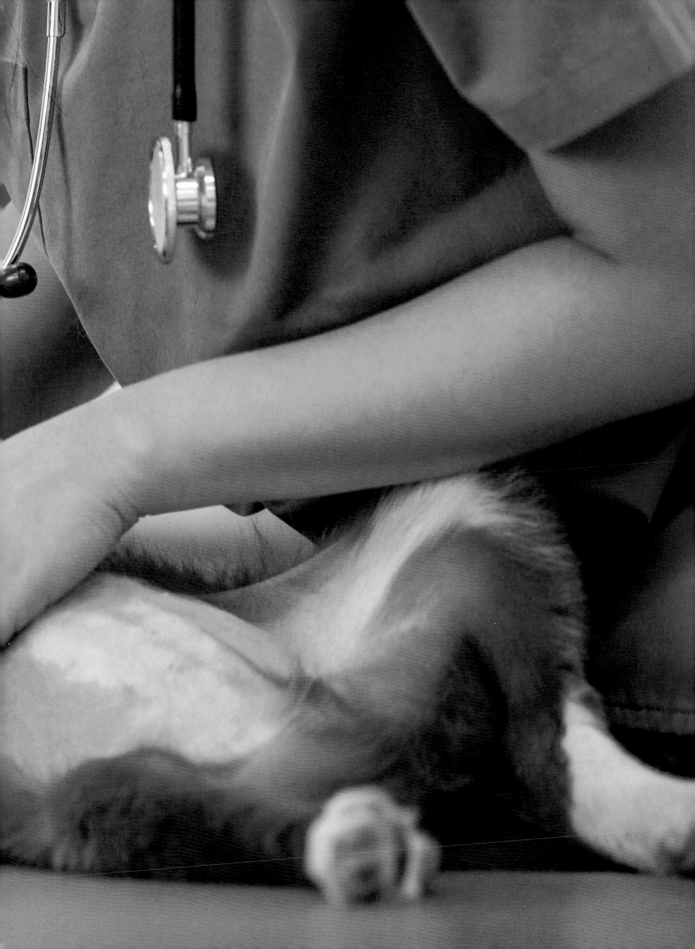

Grooming Basics

Depending on your dog's coat, brushing may be a daily or weekly practice. In general, the longer the dog's fur, the more frequent the grooming.

Grooming should be calming. Begin with briefer and more frequent brushings. Speak in a soothing voice. Be gentle as you follow the direction of the hairs.

Ready, Set, Brush!

Starting at the dog's shoulders, use long, sweeping strokes. The neck, chest, and back are next, then down the body and along the tail. Carefully brush the dog's undersides and legs. Finish by working very gently on the head, ears, and muzzle.

Each part of the coat should receive several strokes of the brush or comb. If fur is tangled or matted, do not tug. Use your fingers to unknot the clump. If it will not separate, ask an adult to help with scissors.

BRUSHES

The coats of different dogs need different tools. A groomer, vet, or breeder can suggest what is right for your dog.

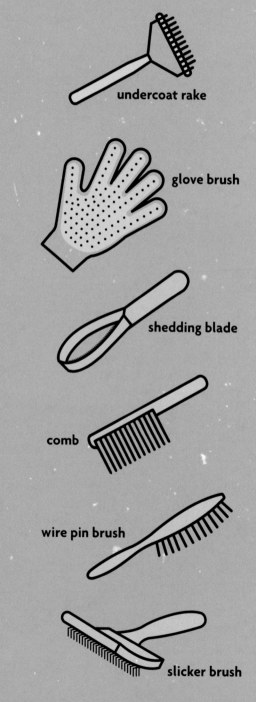

undercoat rake

glove brush

shedding blade

comb

wire pin brush

slicker brush

Dog Prints

Your dog is an important member of your family. Take its paw print to make a card or create a keepsake. If your dog is a puppy, repeat this activity every few months. Watch and see how your dog grows!

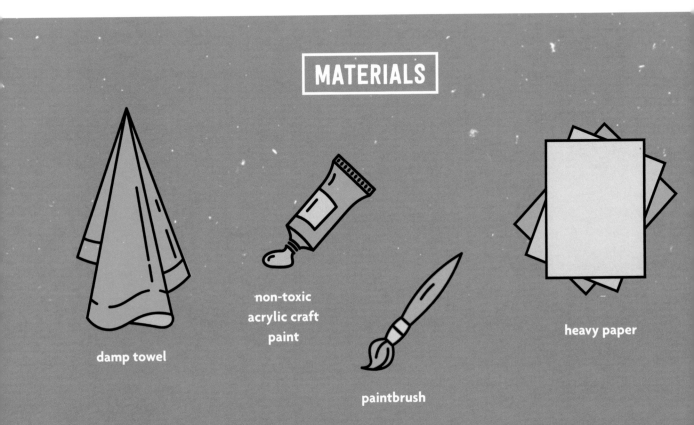

MATERIALS

damp towel

non-toxic acrylic craft paint

paintbrush

heavy paper

1. Wipe off your dog's paw with a damp towel. Clean between the pads, too. Then use the paintbrush to lightly paint the pads only.

2. Gently press the paw to the paper. Hold it there for a few seconds. Carefully lift your dog's paw straight up.

3. While the paint dries, wipe the paint off your dog's paw.

4. Make a card out of your dog's paw print. Or, write the date and your dog's name and age on the paper. Hang it on your fridge. Or put it in a picture frame!

Glossary

anxious: restless, nervous, or worried; an anxious dog will often whine or pant

grooming: caring for the skin and fur by brushing and cleaning it

massage: to rub or knead muscles and joints to ease or reduce pain and stiffness

muzzle: the jaws (mouth) and nose of an animal

reassuringly: in a way that makes one feel less afraid or upset

soothing: calming or comforting

Websites

American Kennel Club: Dog Training Basics
http://www.akc.org/content/dog-training/basics/
Pick up tips for training your dog.

Animal Planet: Dogs
http://www.animalplanet.com/pets/dogs/
Watch videos and read articles to learn more about dogs.

Index

Note: Every effort has been made to ensure that the websites listed above are suitable for children, that they have educational value, and that they contain no inappropriate material. However, because of the nature of the Internet, it is impossible to guarantee that these sites will remain active indefinitely or that their contents will not be altered.